DISCARDED BY
DURHAM COUNTY
LIBRARY

DURHAM COUNTY LIBRARY

OCT 05 2011

DURHAM NC

# The **REAL** Scientist Investigates...
# SOUND

## Peter Riley

SEA-TO-SEA
*Mankato Collingwood London*

# Contents

# Sound all Around

Shut your eyes and what do you notice? The first thing is probably a sound! It might be the sound of breathing, voices, or traffic rumbling, or it might be a loud **bang** that makes you jump! Sounds pop into our ears all the time—but how do they get there? Real scientists know that sounds travel in waves through the air.

Air is made up of tiny particles called atoms and molecules. They're so small you would need a very powerful microscope to see them—think of them as microscopic marbles.

When something goes bang, the first thing that happens is a movement. The tight skin on a drum shakes, a bursting balloon suddenly shrinks, or a wind chime sways in the breeze.

The next thing that happens is a change in the air. Atoms and molecules in the air get shaken up. They crash together and swing back and forth, sending out ripples, or waves, of sound.

When the sound waves reach our ears, they whizz right into our heads. There, our brains make sense of them. The same thing happens with even the quietest sounds. Seems simple? Let's investigate!

# How to Be a Real Scientist

Real scientists look at our world and try to understand it by thinking about it and performing experiments. You can be a real scientist, too! Just look at each topic, read the "Get Going" section, and then start experimenting.

## Set Up a Science Box

Find a large box, then look through the pages in this book to find out all the things you will need in order to get going on each activity. Gather them up and put them in your science box.

## Use These Science Skills

▶ **Observe**
Look carefully at whatever you are investigating.

▶ **Predict**
Guess what will happen before you experiment.

▶ **A fair test**
If you are comparing sounds, make sure you keep everything the same in your tests, except for one thing, such as the type of noisemaker you use, or the distance from the sound to your ear.

▶ **Science notebook**
You will need a science notebook in which to put information about your investigations.

▶ **Record**
Write down what happened and perhaps make a drawing in your science notebook. You could take photographs, too, or make a video using a camcorder or cellphone.

▶ **Make a conclusion**
Compare what actually happened with your prediction and see if you were right. It does not matter if you were wrong because it helps you rethink your ideas.

▶ **Experiments and answers**
Follow the steps in the experiments carefully. Use your science skills. There may be extra experiments and a question for you to try. Check all your observations, ideas, and answers on pages 28–29.

▶ **What went wrong?**
Science experiments are famous for going wrong—sometimes. If your experiment does not seem to work, check the "What's wrong?" section to help you make it right.

# V-v-vibrations

The movements that make sounds are very speedy! They flicker in one direction and then the opposite direction many, many times a second. Real scientists call them vibrations. Most vibrations are so fast we can't see them. If you shut this book quickly, you will hear a quiet bang, but you won't see the pages vibrating.

▼ The louder the sound, the bigger the vibrations. The noise from a jet engine can shake the ground!

Sometimes you can feel a vibration even if you can't see it. Look into a mirror and whistle. Your lips might tingle a little, but you won't see them move as they vibrate the air.

► The wings of a hummingbird flutter so fast it's hard to see they are moving. They make a whirring sound as the air around them vibrates.

## Get Going
Inside your throat are flaps, called vocal cords, that vibrate when you talk or sing. Press your fingers on the front of your throat and hum your favorite tune. Can you feel the vibrations? Now make some vibrations you can see!

**1**

Cut a piece of plastic bag that is a few inches larger than the top of the cookie can.

**2**

Cover the open top of the cookie can with the piece of plastic and secure it in place with the rubber band.

## Science Box

Cookie can about 8 in. (20 cm) wide, lid removed, plastic bag, scissors, large rubber band at least ¼ in. (0.5 cm) thick, sequins (or rice, salt, sugar, scraps of tissue paper), cookie can lid or metal tray, small wooden cutting board, large metal spoon, metal fork with long, thin prongs.

**3**

Firmly but steadily pull the plastic tight in all directions across the top of the cookie can.

**4**

Set the sequins on the plastic. Bring the metal lid to about 4 in. (10 cm) above them and strike the lid with the spoon.

▶ **Observe**
What happens to the sequins when you bang the metal lid? What happens when you bang the lid closer to or farther from the drum?
Repeat the experiment using the wooden cutting board instead of the metal lid. What do you find?

▶ **Predict**
How might the other "jumpers," such as sugar, salt, or tissue paper, react to the bang? Which do you think would move the most? Test your prediction.

▶ **Fair test**
Hit the wooden cutting board with the same strength as you hit the metal tray, and from the same distances.

▶ **What's wrong?**
Jumpers not moving? Hit the tray harder.

▶ **Record**
Use a camcorder to record the movement of the "jumpers" as a friend hits the lid.

▶ **Extra experiment**
Strike the prongs of the fork on the cutting board. What do you see? Lift the fork to your ear with the prongs pointing directly upward (not into your ear and away from your eyes). What do you hear?

# Sound On the Move

Sound travels because vibrations don't just stop where they started. A vibrating object shakes the atoms and molecules next to it, which in turn shake the atoms and molecules next to them. The vibration passes on to particles farther and farther away from the object, creating what real scientists call a sound wave.

▼ Many water animals, such as dolphins, communicate with each other through sound. Their calls carry much farther than they can see.

Sound waves travel straight through stuff, not across the surface like water waves do. In gases, like air, the particles can move freely. In liquids, they are packed closer together but can still move around. In solids, they are held in place but can vibrate a little. In space, or in a vacuum, there are no atoms or molecules, and so there is no sound.

## Get Going

Sound waves travel faster through liquids than they do through gases, and even faster through solids. See if you can hear the difference...

**1** Hold a metal spoon at arm's length and tap it on the end of a table.

**2** Keep your arm outstretched and lower your head so your ear presses against the table top. Tap the spoon again.

# Spoon Tunes

## Science Box

Metal teaspoon, table, string about 20 in. (50 cm) long, large serving spoon, wooden spoon, 2 balloons, jug of water, ruler, ticking clock or watch.

▶ **Observe**
How did the sound of the knocking spoon change when you rested your head on the table top?

▶ **Predict**
Before you try step 4, predict what might happen.

▶ **Record**
Record the sound of the spoon when it is struck on the table edge. Repeat steps 3 and 4 with a large metal serving spoon and a wooden spoon. Describe the different sounds.

▶ **Extra experiment**
Fill a balloon with water and one with air to about 4 in. (10 cm) across and knot them. Place a ticking clock or watch on the table, place each balloon over it in turn, and listen through it. (Don't press the balloons too hard!) Compare the sounds.

▶ **Think about it**
When a star or spaceship explodes in a science fiction movie, should it really go BANG?

**3**

Tie a loop in the middle of the string and insert a teaspoon.

**4**

*Make a prediction before doing this.* Press one end of the string to the outside of your right ear and the other to your left ear. (Don't poke the string in your ears.) Tap the spoon against the table.

# Talking Telephones

With a telephone, you can make sound travel as far as the other side of the world. A telephone has a microphone, which vibrates when you speak into it. The vibrations are changed into tiny currents of electricity, which zoom either through cables or as radio waves all the way to the phone you're calling.

▼ Cellphones use radio waves that can cross both air and space. The loudspeaker vibrates so you can hear who's talking.

At the other end of the line, electrical currents make a loudspeaker in the earpiece vibrate. These vibrations make sound waves in the air, which travel into the listener's ear.

▲ The first telephones used exactly the same loudspeaker and earpiece system as we use today. Only now they are a bit smaller!

## Get Going

In ordinary telephone cables, sound is changed into pulses of light that travel along special fibers. Can you make a simple phone cable out of a piece of string or dental floss? Try it!

**1**

Push the thumbtack into the center of the base of each yogurt container to make a hole. Poke the pencil through the hole to make it bigger.

**2**

Run one end of the string into each hole through the base, and knot each end to a paper clip.

## String-a-ling!

### Science Box

2 clean cardboard yogurt containers or paper cups, thumbtack, pencil, piece of string at least 10 ft. (3 m) long, 2 paperclips, a friend, 2 styrofoam cups, yarn, dental floss.

**3**

Pull the string so the paper clip fits snugly into the bottom of the pot.

**4**

Ask a friend to help you pull the string tightly and speak into the container while you listen to the other.

▶ **Observe**
Cover the ear that's not on the telephone with one hand. Can you hear what your friend is saying more clearly? Can your friend hear what you are saying?

▶ **Predict**
Predict what might happen if you slacken the string and then talk. Test your prediction.

▶ **Record**
Repeat the experiment using styrofoam cups and the same length of string. Can you hear more clearly? Experiment with cups of different sizes. Try yarn, and then dental floss, instead of string. Make a table to record which combination of materials works best.

▶ **What's wrong?**
Can't hear your friend's voice when you try the telephones at first? Pull the string tighter.

▶ **Extra experiment**
Attach a third telephone on a piece of string to the middle of the string between your two telephones. Can a third person join in your conversation?

# ECHO...Echo...Echo

While sound travels easily through most solids, liquids, and gases, it has more trouble moving from one to another. So, when a sound wave shooting through air hits something solid, such as a brick wall, it bounces back. Real scientists call this reflection. Most reflected sounds are too weak or too quick for us to hear, but sometimes we hear one as an echo.

Sound is very fast. It travels 36 yards (33 m) in $\frac{1}{10}$ of a second through air. To hear an echo, you need to stand at least 56 ft. (17 m) from a high wall and then clap your hands. If you stand closer, the echo will reach you too quickly and overlap with your clap.

▼ Bats use echoes to find food. They emit a high-pitched screech. The bat can then tell the distance by how long it takes the echo to bounce back.

▼ Radar is used to monitor aircraft. It sends out radio waves that bounce back off objects in the sky. Each "blip" on this screen is an aircraft.

## Get Going

All surfaces reflect sound, but they absorb some of the energy in sound waves, too. Some surfaces absorb hardly any sound and are good reflectors. Others absorb large amounts and are poor reflectors of sound. Try a test to find out!

# Bouncing Sound

## Science Box

2 cardboard paper towel tubes, metal lid, piece of soft cloth and a sheet of paper to rap around the lid, modeling clay, ticking clock or watch, measuring tape.

**1**

Set up the two tubes at right angles to each other on a table. You can hold them in place with modeling clay. Place the clock or watch at the end of one tube and your ear at the end of the other. Listen for the ticking sound.

**2**

Stand the metal lid near the place where the tubes meet at a right angle and secure it with modeling clay. Listen for the ticking sound again.

▶ **Observe**
Try covering the ear farthest from the tube. What happens? How did the sound change when you put the metal lid in place? How did the sound change when you used the different materials?

▶ **What's wrong?**
Can't hear any difference in the sounds? Try again in a quieter room.

▶ **Extra experiment**
Find a high wall with a large open space in front of it. Stand 3 ft. (1 m) from the wall and clap your hands. Move back 3 ft. (1 m) and repeat. Keep moving back. At what distance can you hear the echo?

**3**

Wrap the cloth around the lid then repeat step 2. Replace the cloth with the paper and try again.

▶ **Think about it**
When a room is being decorated and the furnishings are removed, or a gymnasium is empty, all the sounds there seem louder. Why?

# What a Noise!

Almost everything makes a sound as it moves. But why do some sounds make us want to cover our ears, while others are too quiet to notice? Real scientists know the loudness of a sound depends on the amount of energy used to make it. It also depends how close the listener is to the first vibrations!

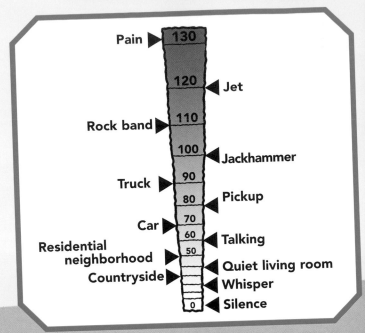

▼ Scientists use a scale to measure the loudness of sounds. It is called the decibel scale.

| | |
|---|---|
| Pain ▶ | 130 |
| | 120 ◀ Jet |
| Rock band ▶ | 110 |
| | 100 ◀ Jackhammer |
| Truck ▶ | 90 |
| | 80 ◀ Pickup |
| Car ▶ | 70 |
| | 60 ◀ Talking |
| Residential neighborhood ▶ | 50 |
| | ◀ Quiet living room |
| Countryside ▶ | ◀ Whisper |
| | 0 ◀ Silence |

## Get Going

The more energy that goes into a sound, the louder it is and the farther it travels. Say a word, then shout it. Which uses more energy? Which makes the loudest sound? Now let's try making some noise.

▲ The sound of a racing car is very loud as it races around a track, but as it drives farther away, it seems quieter.

# Sound Shakers

**1**

Take a container and fill it enough to cover the bottom with one of the shaking materials.

## Science Box

Collection of containers with lids (yogurt containers, plastic cups, cardboard tubes), shaking materials (rice, paper clips, buttons, fish-tank gravel), adhesive tape, MP3 player or other sound-recording device, yardstick (1 m ruler), 2 metal oven pans (one smaller than the other).

**3**

Set up your sound-recording device 1 yard (1 m) away and make as large a sound as you can with the shaker.

**2**

Close the container and seal it tightly. Rattle it first with slow, small shakes then increase the speed and size of the shakes.

**4**

Try different combinations of container and shaking material. Repeat steps 1–3 to find the combination that makes the loudest sound.

▶ **Observe**
How did the sound change as you shook the shaker faster and more strongly?
Listen to all the recordings in turn and decide which makes the loudest sound.

▶ **Record**
Make your own "loudness" scale, listing your shakers from loudest to quietest.

▶ **Fair test**
Make sure you record each shaker at its loudest and the same distance from the microphone.

▶ **Extra experiment**
Place the larger metal tray on a hard floor. Hold the other tray 4 in. (10 cm) above it, then let go. Repeat with the tray at 8 in. (20 cm) and 12 in. (30 cm) above the larger metal tray. What will happen if you drop it from your waist or higher? Test your prediction.

▶ **Think about it**
Stand by an open door and listen to the noises in your neighborhood for a minute every hour. Estimate the loudness level using the decibel scale to help you. When were the loudest times?

# In-shhhh-ulation!

A really loud sound roaring in your ears can damage your hearing and even make you sick. Some machines are loud because their tough metal parts grind together, so special materials have been developed to absorb some of the energy of the sound waves. These sound mufflers are called insulating materials.

▼ The walls of a music recording studio are covered with insulating materials to absorb the sound.

▼ Protective earphones block out loud sounds that could permanently damage these workers' hearing.

Some machines get so hot when they are working that any insulated covering would catch fire. Ear protectors made of insulating material help to reduce the power of sounds reaching people's ears.

## Get Going

Are your hands good sound insulators? Turn on a radio and play it quietly, then put your hands over your ears to check your answer. Now test some other materials to see how well they muffle sound.

**1**

Switch on the noise-maker. Put it in the empty container and close the lid.

### Science Box

A noisemaker such as a buzzing egg timer or alarm clock, a container (with a lid) big enough to hold the noisemaker and insulation, cotton balls, measuring tape, pieces of newspaper scrunched up into balls, bubble wrap, polystyrene loose fill, MP3 player or other sound-recording device.

**2**

**3**

Walk away from the box until you can no longer hear the sound. Measure how far you have walked.

Record the sound coming from the box at a distance of 3 ft. (1 m).

▶ **Observe**
How far did you have to walk during the test for each insulator? Listen to the recordings made from 3 ft. (1m) away for each material. How do they compare?

▶ **Fair test**
Make sure the box is packed with material for each test.

▶ **Record**
From your results in step 2, arrange the sound-insulating materials in order, starting with the one that absorbed the most sound. Using your results in step 3, do the same. How do the results compare?

▶ **Predict**
Use your arrangement of insulating materials as an insulation scale. Predict where on the scale a T-shirt would come if you wrapped it around the alarm clock and put it in the box. Test your prediction.

▶ **Think about it**
What is the shape of loud sound waves? Think of a rough sea and then draw some waves. Imagine these rough waves going through an insulating material and coming out the other side. Draw how they have changed.

**4**

Open the box and pack the cotton balls in around the noisemaker, then close the lid again. Repeat steps 2 and 3. Repeat the test using the other insulating materials.

# Up High, Down Low!

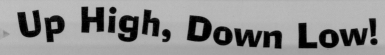

Listen to the sounds around you. There are many different kinds. Some sounds are high like a "ping," others are lower, more like a "pong." Real scientists call the ping or pong of a sound its pitch. Pitch helps us identify sounds and tell one apart from another.

Scientists have invented a machine called an oscilloscope that lets us see what sound waves look like. This shows that high sounds make lots of short waves, while low sounds make fewer, longer waves.

▲ When the microphone of an oscilloscope vibrates with a sound, it creates electrical currents that make the sound waves appear on a screen.

▶ The bars of a xylophone produce notes of different pitch when a player strikes them with a stick or mallet.

## Get Going

High-pitched sound waves are said to have a high frequency, while low-pitched waves have a low frequency. How many different sound frequencies can you create? Let's play with frequency and pitch!

18

# Bottle Xylophone

**1** Gently tap each bottle with the pencil and arrange them in order, starting with the one that makes the sound with the highest pitch.

### Science Box

Collection of glass bottles in which two of the bottles are the same, jug of water, pencil, MP3 player or other sound-recording device.

**2** Half fill each bottle with water and tap them again. Do they still make sounds in the same order of pitch?

**3** Empty a large bottle and fill up the one that is next to it in your arrangement. Tap the bottles again and compare.

**4** Take the two similar bottles and fill one two-thirds full of water and the other one-third full of water. Tap each one, then blow across the top of each one.

### ▶ Observe
How did the pitch arrangement change in step 2? What changes did you notice in steps 3 and 4? How did the sound change when you blew across the tops of the bottles instead of tapping them?

### ▶ Record
Use an MP3 player to record your investigations.

### ▶ Extra equipment
Arrange your bottles in order of pitch and try to play a tune. You could change the amounts of water and try to tune them to the notes on a keyboard.

### ▶ Think about it
Why do long sound waves have a lower frequency than short waves?

# Sound Makes Sound!

Have you ever tried to push someone on a swing out of time? It doesn't work very well. The swing moves best at its own natural rhythm, or frequency. Every object has a frequency at which it vibrates. When that sound frequency reaches the object, the object begins to shake and produce sound, too. Real scientists call this resonance.

Resonating objects can be used to amplify sound, in other words, make them louder. Many speaker systems work in this way. One part vibrates, another part joins in, and so the sound increases.

## Get Going

An object's natural frequency depends on its size and shape. Hold a long ruler by one end and twang the other. Try the same with a short ruler. Do you notice a difference? Now make a model to find out for yourself how resonance works.

▲ When an earthquake shakes the ground at a certain frequency, buildings with the same natural frequency tremble more and may collapse. This is resonance in terrifying action!

**1** Make each paper strip into a ring and join the ends with adhesive tape.

## Science Box

4 strips of paper, each 1 in. (2.5 cm) wide with lengths of 20 in. (50 cm), 16 in. (42 cm), 13 in. (34 cm), and 10 in. (26 cm), piece of cardboard at least 8 x 6 in. (20 x 15 cm), adhesive tape, 2 same-sized plastic bottles

**2** Stick each ring to the cardboard in order of size, starting with the largest at one end.

**3** Place the cardboard on a flat surface and move it very slowly backward and forward.

**4** Move the cardboard faster back and forth. Keep increasing the speed and making the distance the cardboard moves shorter.

▶ **Observe**
What happens when you move the cardboard slowly? What happens as you increase the speed of the movement? What happens when you move the cardboard as fast as you can?

▶ **Fair test**
Make another set of rings including two the same size. What do you notice when you move them as above?

▶ **Extra equipment**
Hold a bottle in front of your mouth and one a couple of inches from an ear. Make a "pooh, pooh" sound into the bottle and listen to the bottle by your ear.

▶ **Think about it**
Why were resonators used in Greek and Roman theaters?

# Blow Me a Tune!

If you play a musical instrument, you're already an expert in frequency and pitch! Wind instruments produce sounds when a player blows into them. Holes in the side of the instrument can be opened or closed, changing the length and frequency of the sound waves inside. This creates notes of different pitch, which can be used to play a tune.

Recorders, flutes, trombones, and clarinets are just a few types of wind instrument. They create different sounds and are played in different ways, but they all make music through air vibrating inside a tube.

▼ **This man is playing a didgeridoo. This musical instrument has a very low frequency.**

## Get Going
Panpipes are an ancient type of wind instrument made from a series of tubes. You can create some out of drinking straws! Try making a reed mouthpiece, like an oboe has, too.

**1**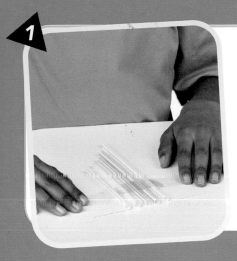

Cut straws to the following lengths in inches: 7, 6, 5½, 5, 4½, 4, 3½, 3 (17.5, 15.5, 13.5, 12.5, 11, 10, 9, and 8.5 cm). Stick the straws along the poster board, starting with the longest. Leave a gap of about a straw's width between them.

## Science Box

Plastic straws, scissors, ruler, piece of poster board about 6½ x 5 in. (16 x 12 cm), adhesive tape.

**2**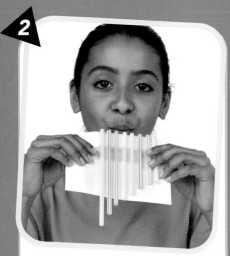

Put the poster board below your lower lip and blow across each straw one at a time.

**3**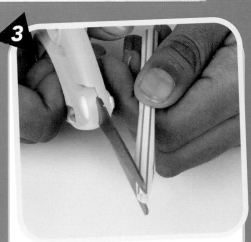

Take another straw and flatten about ¾ in. (2 cm) of one end. Cut away the sides for about ½ in. (1 cm) to make a blunt V-shape. This is a reed.

▶ **Observe**
How do the sounds differ from straw to straw? Can you make the straws match musical notes on a keyboard? Repeat step 4 but gently bite the straw about 1¼ in. (3 cm) from the end and blow. Move the straw in and out of your mouth a little. What do you hear?

▶ **Extra experiment**
Cut some more straws to different lengths and give each one a reed. Blow each one at a time and hear how their sounds compare.

▶ **What's wrong?**
Can't get a note with the reed? Flatten the end more. Blow very gently at first and gradually increase the strength of your blow. It may take a few tries to make a sound.

▶ **Predict**
Imagine dipping the end of a straw in a plastic cup of water and gently blowing across the top. How would the sound change if you lowered the straw deeper into the water and blew again? Try it out to check your answer.

**4**

Put the reed in your mouth and gently close your lips over the straw about 1¼ in. (3 cm) from the end. Blow through the straw.

# Singing Strings

Ping a set of strings and you can make more music! String instruments vary widely, from violins and cellos to harps, banjos, and guitars. They all have strings of different thicknesses, stretched across a hollow box or frame. A player either plucks the strings, strums them, or scrapes them with a bow. Each string produces a different note.

▼ An electric guitar uses an electrical amplifier to increase the sounds made by the strings.

The range of notes can be increased by pressing down on a string in different places. This changes the string's tightness at the point where it is played.

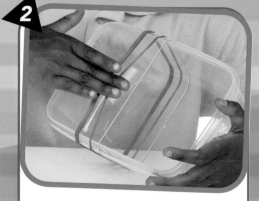

**1**

**2**

## Get Going
If anyone you know has a stringed instrument, ask if you can try to play it. You can also make your own guitar out of a plastic box with some rubber bands.

Stretch the rubber bands around the plastic box, about ½ in. (1 cm) apart, starting with the thickest. Make sure the bands are not twisted.

Pluck each band in turn. Stroke a finger or thumb across them so that you get them all to sound quickly, one after another.

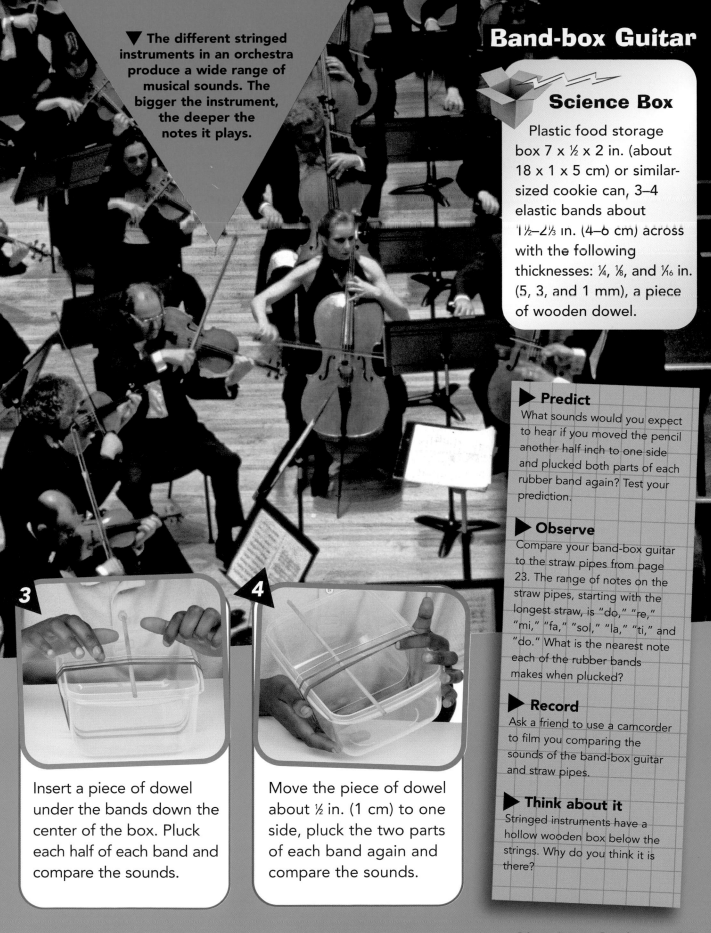

The different stringed instruments in an orchestra produce a wide range of musical sounds. The bigger the instrument, the deeper the notes it plays.

# Band-box Guitar

## Science Box

Plastic food storage box 7 x ½ x 2 in. (about 18 x 1 x 5 cm) or similar-sized cookie can, 3–4 elastic bands about 1½–2⅓ in. (4–6 cm) across with the following thicknesses: ¼, ⅛, and ¹⁄₁₆ in. (5, 3, and 1 mm), a piece of wooden dowel.

▶ **Predict**
What sounds would you expect to hear if you moved the pencil another half inch to one side and plucked both parts of each rubber band again? Test your prediction.

▶ **Observe**
Compare your band-box guitar to the straw pipes from page 23. The range of notes on the straw pipes, starting with the longest straw, is "do," "re," "mi," "fa," "sol," "la," "ti," and "do." What is the nearest note each of the rubber bands makes when plucked?

▶ **Record**
Ask a friend to use a camcorder to film you comparing the sounds of the band-box guitar and straw pipes.

▶ **Think about it**
Stringed instruments have a hollow wooden box below the strings. Why do you think it is there?

**3**
Insert a piece of dowel under the bands down the center of the box. Pluck each half of each band and compare the sounds.

**4**
Move the piece of dowel about ½ in. (1 cm) to one side, pluck the two parts of each band again and compare the sounds.

# Hear Ear!

Sounds are only sounds because we can hear them with our ears. Our ears let sound waves into our head, to be translated by our brain. There are three parts to the ear—the outer, middle, and inner ear. The outer ear is the only part we can see. It gathers sound waves and directs them to the working parts inside.

▼ The sound waves travel through the ear canal to a thin sheet called the eardrum. This passes the vibrations to three tiny bones in the middle ear, which make the vibrations stronger.

**Ear canal**

**Middle ear**

**Ear bones**

**Inner ear**

**Cochlea**

**Eardrum**

**Outer ear**

In the inner ear, the sound waves hit a liquid that sends vibrations whizzing through a curly tube called the cochlea. Tiny hairs in the cochlea start to sway and send messages along nerves to the brain. The brain then figures out what the sound is.

▲ This fennec fox has massive outer ears to help it detect quiet sounds made by its prey.

## Get Going

Our two ears work together to gather sounds from all around us. What would happen if one ear was damaged? Try an experiment to change how your ears hear sound.

**1**

Sit on a chair and close your eyes. Ask a friend to move around you, about 6 ft. (2 m) away, and click the coins. After each click, point to where you think you heard them. Cover each ear in turn and repeat.

## Science Box

2 coins, a chair, a friend, piece of poster board about 16 x 12 in. (40 x 30 cm), large paper clip, adhesive tape, scissors, MP3 player or other sound-recording device.

**2**

Fold the poster board to make a cone and secure it with a large paperclip. Use a strip of adhesive tape to join the overlap.

**3**

Cut off the pointed end of the cone so it fits over your ear hole but does not go inside it.

**4**

Ask a friend to whisper to you from a distance of about 3 ft. (1 m) away without using your ear trumpet and again with your ear trumpet in place.

▶ **Observe**
How accurate were you at identifying sound direction with both ears, your left ear, and your right ear? How did the hearing of the whisper change when you used your ear trumpet?

▶ **Predict**
Whisper at the microphone of a sound-recording device from about 3 ft. (1 m) away. Predict what will happen when you put the ear trumpet around the microphone and repeat the process. Test your prediction.

▶ **Extra equipment**
Set up the drum from page 7, put some rice on it and hit a spoon on a metal lid about 4 in. (10 cm) above it. Now cut a slit across the drum about 2 in. (5 cm) long, hit the lid, and watch the rice again. Predict what will happen if the slit is made longer, then try it.

▶ **Think about it**
In some ear diseases, the ear bones stop moving. What happens to a person with this condition?

# Results and Answers

## Page 7 Make It Jump!

You should feel your vocal cords vibrating. When you hit the lid, some of the sequins directly under where it was hit moved up and down. The closer the source of the noise is to the drum, the higher the sequins jump. The wooden block creates weaker vibrations than the metal tray. Sugar and salt may jump the most because they are the lightest. The prongs of the fork vibrate too fast to be seen but they make a faint humming sound.

## Page 9 Spoon Tunes

The sound of the knocking spoon is loudest and strongest when your ear is resting on the table top. When you hold the string to your ears, sound travels along the string and you will hear a "ring," like a bell. All metal spoons sound like bells, but with the wooden spoon, you will hear a "thud" sound. In the extra experiment, you will hear the sound of the clock more clearly through the water balloon than the one filled with air. Think about it—there should not be the sound of the explosion traveling through space because there is nothing for sound to travel through!

## Page 11 String-a-ling!

You and your friend should be able to hear each other. If you cover the ear that's not on the telephone, you'll be able to hear your friend's voice more clearly because the noise of other sounds is reduced. The sound will not travel down the slack string because the atoms and molecules in it cannot vibrate to produce sound waves. The styrofoam cups make a weaker sound because tiny air pockets are trapped between the styrofoam material, which reduce the speed of the vibrations and the number of sound waves. Larger cups should make a clearer sound because they produce more vibrations (they are made of more material). String may work better than yarn or dental floss because it vibrates more when pulled tight. In the extra experiment, a third person would be able to listen to your messages and join in the conversation provided the strings were tight.

## Page 13 Bouncing Sound

You can hear more clearly through the tube when your other ear is covered. The sound was loudest when the metal lid was in place and quietest when the soft cloth was in place. You should hear an echo when you are more than 18 yards (17 m) away from the wall. Furnishings have soft surfaces, which absorb sound. Hard surfaces of walls without paper reflect more sound.

## Page 15 Sound Shakers

Shouting takes more energy and makes a louder sound than speaking. The contents that are large, have hard surfaces, and can move—shaken strongly in the container with the hardest surface—make the loudest sounds. The greater the height of the tray, the more energy it has to rush to the floor and the louder the crashing sound it makes. The morning and evening rush hours may be the noisiest times of the day because of all the traffic.

## Page 17 Can You Hear It Now?

The hands act as sound-insulating materials. Material with a soft, rough surface will absorb the most sound. The T-shirt may come in the middle of the scale. The loud sound waves have high crests with deep troughs between them. After they have passed through the insulating material, they should have low crests and shallow troughs between them (see page 30).

## Page 19 Bottle Xylophone

The smallest bottle should have the highest pitch. When the bottles have water in them, their pitch should be lower because there is more material (glass and water) to vibrate, but they should still be in the same order of pitch. Blowing across the bottle top makes the column of air in the bottle vibrate. It has a lower pitch. Water in the bottle shortens the air column and raises the pitch. Frequency is a measure of how quickly sound waves pass by. Longer sound waves take longer to pass by than shorter sound waves and so have lower frequency.

## Page 21 Resonant Rings

In "Get Going," the long ruler vibrates at a lower frequency than the short ruler. Your observations will include that the larger ring vibrates at the lowest frequency. As the frequency increases (when the speed increases but the distance reduces), the larger ring stops vibrating. The smallest ring vibrates at the fastest frequency. Two rings of the same size and material vibrate at the same frequency. In the extra experiment, the second bottle near your ear resonates and makes a sound. In ancient theaters, resonators amplified the voices of the actors so the audience could hear them more clearly.

## Page 23 Straw Pipes

The pitch of the piped notes rises as you move from the longest to the shortest straw. The pitch lowers when you move from the shortest to the longest straw. The straws play the following notes starting with the longest—do, re, mi, fa, sol, la, ti, do. The straw should make a squeaky trumpeting sound when the reed is blown. When you slide the straw out between your teeth the pitch of the sound rises. When you draw it in, the pitch lowers. When you lower a straw into water and blow across its top, the pitch rises.

## Page 25 Band-box Guitar

The thickest rubber band produces the lowest-pitched note and the thinnest rubber band produces the highest. When the rubber bands are stretched by the piece of dowel, they give a higher pitch. Moving the dowel makes the shorter length higher in pitch and the longer length lower. The hollow box acts as a resonator, making the sound of the strings louder by reflecting sound waves out of the box.

## Page 27 Listen Very Carefully

Both ears are used to locate sound, so if one is damaged or covered up it is more difficult to tell where a sound is coming from. The ear trumpet makes whispers easier to hear. The cut drum does not vibrate, and a longer slit will reduce the vibrations further. (If an ear drum becomes torn a similar thing happens and the hearing is damaged.) When the bones in the ear do not move, a person becomes deaf in that ear.

# Further Information

## Look at these web sites for more information on sound and how we hear things:

▶ http://pbskids.org/zoom/activities/ sci/supersoundingdrums.html
Make a selection of drums at this web site, but make sure an adult is there to help you because you need a blow dryer.

▶ http://www.guardian.co.uk/science/2008/ may/02/physics8?gusrc=rss&feed=science
Follow the simple steps to make an ear gong.

▶ http://home.howstuffworks.com/science-projects-for-kids-producing-sounds1.htm
Try making this model to show how particles move in the air to create sound waves.

▶ http://www.cardiganshirecoastand country.com/dolphin.htm
Bats and dolphins send out sounds we cannot hear and use the reflected sound to help them find food. This process is called echolocation. Hear some of the sounds a dolphin makes at this web site.

▶ http://www.explorelearning.com/index.cfm? method=cResource.dspDetail&ResourceID=32
You can see how particles in the air move with changing frequencies by launching the gizmo at this web site.

▶ http://www.squiglysplayhouse.com/ ArtsAndCrafts/Crafts/Kazoo.html
Make a kazoo by following the instructions on this web page.

▶ http://pbskids.org/zoom/activities/sci/ guitar.html
Make guitars from different kinds of boxes with the investigation on this web site.

▶ http://id.mind.net/~zona/mstm/physics/waves/ partsOfAWave/waveParts.htm#pictureOfAWave
You can see how to change the frequency of a wave by scrolling down to the bottom of this web site screen and moving the blue button to the right and left.

Every effort has been made by the Publishers to ensure that these web sites contain no inappropriate or offensive material. However, because of the nature of the Internet, it is impossible to guarantee that the contents of these sites will not be altered. We strongly advise that Internet access is supervised by a responsible adult.

# Glossary

**Absorb (sound)**
To take in the energy in sound waves.

**Atoms**
Very tiny objects, often called particles, that make up all materials.

**Decibel**
A unit used in the measurement of the loudness of sound.

**Echo**
A copy of a sound made by the reflection of the original sound.

**Frequency**
The number of waves that pass by in a certain amount of time, such as a second.

**Insulator (sound)**
A material that reduces the amount of sound passing through it.

**Molecules**
Very tiny objects or particles made up from groups of atoms.

**Monitor**
To check on the position and number of things, such as aircraft, in a particular place.

**Note (music)**
A sound of a certain pitch and length, which is made by the voice or musical instruments.

**Particles**
Very tiny objects such as atoms and molecules.

**Pitch**
The highness ("ping") or lowness ("pong") of a sound.

**Pulses**
Tiny "packets" of energy, such as small flashes of light.

**Radar**
The letters stand for Radio Detection And Ranging, in which radio waves are sent out in all directions and their reflections are gathered and displayed on a screen.

**Reflect**
To change the direction of a sound, radio, or light wave so that it goes back to its source.

**Resonance**
The vibration of an object at the same frequency as a source of sound so that the object makes the sound, too.

**Sound wave**
The regular way in which a sound moves through solid, liquid, or gas, when particles in the material sway from side to side.

**Vacuum**
A place where there aren't any particles of matter that make up solids, liquids, or gases. Vacuums are found in space.

**Vibration**
A rapid backward and forward or up and down shaking movement.

# Index

To my granddaughter Pippa May

This edition first published in 2011 by
Sea-to-Sea Publications
Distributed by Black Rabbit Books
P.O. Box 3263, Mankato, Minnesota 56002

Text copyright © Peter Riley 2008, 2011
Design and concept © Sea-to-Sea
Publications 2011
Printed in China, Dongguan
All rights reserved.

Library of Congress Cataloging-in-Publication Data

Riley, Peter D.
   Sound / Peter Riley.
      p. cm. -- (The real scientist investigates)
   Includes index.
   ISBN 978-1-59771-283-5 (lib. bdg.)
   1. Sound--Juvenile literature. I. Title.
   QC225.5.R554 2011
   534.078--dc22
                                    2010005374

9 8 7 6 5 4 3 2

Published by arrangement with the Watts
Publishing Group Ltd., London.

Editor: Susie Brooks
Series Editor: Adrian Cole
Art Director: Jonathan Hair
Design: Matthew Lilly
Picture Research: Diana Morris
Photography: Andy Crawford (unless
otherwise credited)

Acknowledgments:
Ace Stock/Alamy: 12b. Andrey
TTL/Shutterstock: front cover tl. Arvind
Balaraman/Shutterstock: 4t. Hagit
Berkovich/Shutterstock: 26b.
Bettmann/Corbis10b. Yanik Chauvin
/Shutterstock: 2tc, 6b. Mark
Downey/Alamy: 20. Stephen Frink/Corbis:
1b, 2cr, 8-9. Laurence Gough/Shutterstock:
2tl, 5t. Hauhu/Shutterstock: front cover tr.
Inacio Pires/Shutterstock: 10t. Lebrecht
Music and Arts Photo Library /Alamy: 24. J
de Meester/Arco Images/Alamy: 1t, 2bl,
12t, 13t. Marek Mnich/Shutterstock: 3bl,
23. Moodboard/Corbis: 3tl, 16t. Nucleus
Medical Art, Inc/Alamy: 26t. Pictures
Colour Library/Alamy: 3cr, 18b, 22. Caitalin
Plesa/Shutterstock: front cover cl.
qaphotos/Alamy: 16b.
Sciencephotos/Alamy: 3tr, 18t. Perov
Stanislav/Shutterstock: front cover bl.
Stephen Strathdee/Shutterstock: 6t.
Miroslav Tolimir/Shutterstock: front cover
br. Yamato Drummers of Japan: 4b. Robert
Young/Shutterstock: 2br, 14.
*Every attempt has been made to clear copyright.
Should there be any inadvertent omission please
apply to the publisher for rectification.*

March 2010
RD/6000006414/002